Tough Beginnings

How Baby Animals Survive

Marilyn Singer

ILLUSTRATED BY Anna Vojtech

HENRY HOLT AND COMPANY — NEW YORK

Many thanks to Steve Aronson, Paula R. Arms, Dr. Joe Benshemesh, Moe Guertin,
Mary LeCroy, Dorothy Hinshaw Patent, Eric Quinter, Roland Smith, Louis Sorkin,
Kim Vanderlaan, Anna Vojtech, Hans Walter, my editor Christy Ottaviano,
and the crew at Henry Holt and Company

Henry Holt and Company, LLC
Publishers since 1866
115 West 18th Street, New York, New York 10011

Henry Holt is a registered trademark of Henry Holt and Company, LLC
Text copyright © 2001 by Marilyn Singer
Illustrations copyright © 2001 by Anna Vojtech
All rights reserved.
Published in Canada by Fitzhenry & Whiteside Ltd.,
195 Allstate Parkway, Markham, Ontario L3R 4T8.

Library of Congress Cataloging-in-Publication Data
Singer, Marilyn. Tough beginnings: how baby animals survive /
Marilyn Singer; illustrated by Anna Vojtech.
Summary: Presents information about some of the difficulties
faced by different baby animals as they grow to adulthood.
1. Animals—Infancy—Juvenile literature. [1. Animals—Infancy.]
I. Vojtech, Anna, ill. II. Title.   QL763.S54 2001   591.3'9—dc21   00-24282

ISBN 0-8050-6164-9 / First Edition—2001
Designed by Donna Mark
Printed in the United States of America on acid-free paper. ∞
1   3   5   7   9   10   8   6   4   2

The artist used watercolor on Arches paper
to create the illustrations for this book.

To Danny, Linda, Jody, Sarah, and Jonathan Siker

—M. S.

For Tadeas, Martina, and all the other brave newborns

—A. V.

It's tough to begin on the beaches...

There aren't a lot of hiding places on a beach. So a mother sea turtle has to dig a hole in the sand. In it, she lays lots of eggs. Some *species*—types—of turtles lay as many as two hundred of them. Dogs, birds, crabs, lizards, and other predators often eat the eggs or the babies when they hatch. To survive, the tiny turtles must race across the beach as fast as they can to the sea, where they will spend the rest of their lives.

Sometimes they get confused by electric lights on the shore and never reach the water. The ones that do reach it are threatened by new enemies, such as sharks and other large fish. Out of all the babies born, only one in a hundred will become an adult. For some species, it may be one in a thousand. That's a tough beginning!

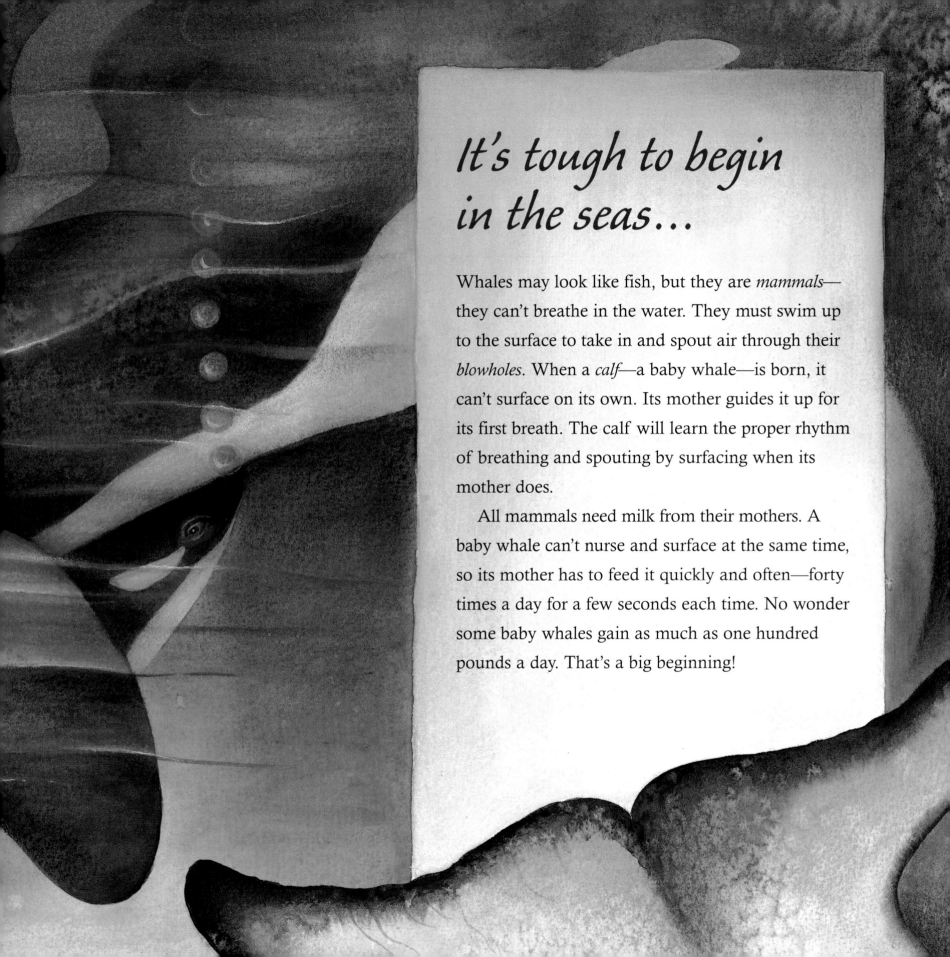

It's tough to begin in the seas...

Whales may look like fish, but they are *mammals*—they can't breathe in the water. They must swim up to the surface to take in and spout air through their *blowholes*. When a *calf*—a baby whale—is born, it can't surface on its own. Its mother guides it up for its first breath. The calf will learn the proper rhythm of breathing and spouting by surfacing when its mother does.

All mammals need milk from their mothers. A baby whale can't nurse and surface at the same time, so its mother has to feed it quickly and often—forty times a day for a few seconds each time. No wonder some baby whales gain as much as one hundred pounds a day. That's a big beginning!

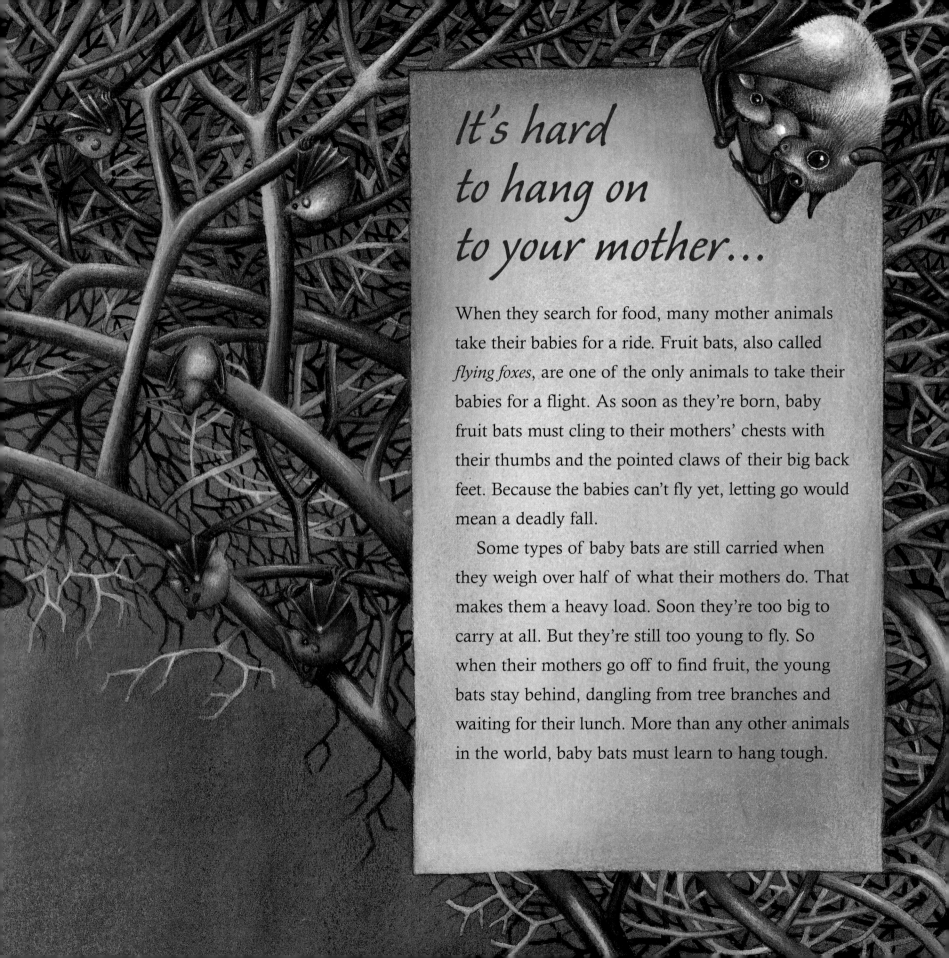

It's hard to hang on to your mother...

When they search for food, many mother animals take their babies for a ride. Fruit bats, also called *flying foxes*, are one of the only animals to take their babies for a flight. As soon as they're born, baby fruit bats must cling to their mothers' chests with their thumbs and the pointed claws of their big back feet. Because the babies can't fly yet, letting go would mean a deadly fall.

Some types of baby bats are still carried when they weigh over half of what their mothers do. That makes them a heavy load. Soon they're too big to carry at all. But they're still too young to fly. So when their mothers go off to find fruit, the young bats stay behind, dangling from tree branches and waiting for their lunch. More than any other animals in the world, baby bats must learn to hang tough.

It's hard to jump out of the trees...

All ducks end up in the water. But they don't begin there. Most start in nests on the ground. Wood ducks nest in tree holes—the higher, the better. A female wood duck lays an average of twelve eggs. About twenty-four hours after they hatch, she calls the ducklings to leave the nest. Each duckling must spring up to the tree hole's entrance, then jump down to the ground below. Sometimes the drop is more than sixty feet. Amazingly, the babies are rarely hurt by the fall.

More dangerous is the trip to the water. It may take the mother duck and her brood as long as a day to reach a good pond, lake, or river. Along the way, there may be predators, automobiles, roadblocks, and other hazards. The babies probably won't all survive. But the ones that do will get to raise their own troop of daring high divers.

It's rough to have too many siblings...

How many sisters and brothers are too many? Ten? Fifteen? Twenty? A mother Virginia opossum—the common opossum of North America—can give birth to as many as fifty babies at one time. The problem is the mother has just thirteen nipples to provide milk for her young. Only the strongest babies manage to find a nipple and nurse. The others die of starvation.

Opossums are *marsupials*—animals with pouches. The mother opossum's nipples are in her pouch. Each baby fastens on to a nipple and doesn't let go for about two months. Once they leave the pouch, the youngsters ride on their mother's back or follow her when she searches for food. Only half of the young survivors are likely to become adult opossums. The others may be eaten by predators, hit by automobiles, or die of disease.

Why does a Virginia opossum have so many babies? Probably to make sure that enough of them will grow up to have too many babies of their own.

It's rough when you're born in a mound...

All birds lay eggs. And all eggs need to be kept warm to hatch. Lots of birds sit on their eggs to incubate them. But not the Australian mallee fowl. A male and female pair dig a huge pit in the ground and fill it with dirt, sand, and leaves. The leaves rot and give off heat, turning the nest into an oven. Over the course of four months, the female lays up to thirty eggs. The male tests the temperature of the nest with his beak and tongue. He keeps it at a steady 92 degrees Fahrenheit by adding or removing the dirt, sand, and rotting leaves.

When the chicks hatch, they must climb out of the three-foot-high pile all by themselves. Some won't make it—especially if the top layer of the mound has baked hard. The ones that do get out will be able to rest for a day in the shade. Then they have to find their own food. All work and no play help baby mallee fowl live to be tough old birds.

It's not easy when Dad wants to eat you...

Some animals will eat almost anything that moves—including their babies. Komodo dragons are among them. They are *cannibals*—they will eat their own kind. A mother Komodo dragon may occasionally guard her eggs, but once they hatch, the baby lizards have to take care of themselves. Their parents don't recognize the babies as their own. To avoid running into predators, including Mom and Dad, the baby Komodo dragons spend most of their time in trees, where they eat insects, birds, and smaller lizards.

When they get older, the young lizards come down to the ground to feed on larger animals, such as goats, deer, and boar. Komodo dragons often feast together. At a meal, the youngsters use special movements to show they know their place and will wait their turn to eat. If the movements don't work and the adult lizards threaten them, the youngsters leave quickly. After all, no young Komodo dragon wants to end up as anyone's dinner—not even Mom's or Dad's.

It's not easy to hide underground...

Like people, cicadas have a long childhood. Unlike people, cicadas spend theirs underground. Periodical cicadas hatch up in trees, then fall to the ground. To avoid being eaten by enemies, these newborn insects, called *nymphs*, must burrow one to three feet into the earth. There, depending on the type of periodical cicada they are, they'll spend the next thirteen or seventeen years of their lives, feeding on juices from tree roots.

After all those years, the nymphs dig their way up and climb into the trees. Their hard outer layer splits, and the soft adult cicadas emerge. Cicadas have no defenses for several minutes until their new covering hardens and their new wings expand and grow firm. Some will get caught by predators, but others will live to sing the familiar buzzing songs we hear every summer.

It's trouble to hatch where it's frozen...

Most birds hatch in warm weather. But not emperor penguin chicks. They hatch in the middle of winter on the Antarctic ice, where the temperature can drop to minus 70 degrees. There are no materials to build nests, and the penguin eggs would freeze if they rested on the ice. So each father penguin *incubates*—warms and hatches—a single egg on his feet, covering it with his special belly flap, called a *brood pouch*.

Soon after the chicks hatch, their mothers return from the sea to provide both food and warmth. The fathers, who haven't eaten in two months, go off to feed. They return in three weeks to help care for the chicks. When the young penguins are bigger, they gather in groups with other chicks for protection from the cold. When they're old enough to swim and fish, the young penguins will face new dangers, this time from seals and polar bears. It's such a tough childhood that only one emperor chick out of five will live past its first birthday. But the lucky survivors will grow up to be the tallest and fattest penguins in the whole world.

It's trouble to hatch where it's dry...

Tadpoles—baby frogs and toads—always start their life in the water. But it's not easy to find water in the southwestern United States. Right after a storm, male and female western spadefoot toads mate in puddles of rainwater. The eggs hatch quickly, and the spadefoot tadpoles change into toads faster than any other species in the world—sometimes in just nine days. They have to change rapidly, or else their homes may dry up before they're ready to leave them.

Spadefoot tadpoles will work together in groups, wiggling to deepen their water hole or to stir up food from the bottom. They'll also eat the tadpoles that have died. When they've at last become toads, they will all leave together—but then they'll go their separate ways. Each toad will find a good spot for a deep burrow. Using its spadelike hind legs, it will dig a cool escape from the hot desert sun.

It's tricky to search for a safe pouch...

Grown-up gray kangaroos—which may be brown or gray—are taller than grown-up people. But newborn gray kangaroos, called *joeys*, are smaller than your thumb. They're also blind and naked and can't move their legs. Yet like all marsupials these babies have to travel from their mother's birth canal to her pouch. How do they do it? They use their tiny arms to push through her fur. This trip is only a few inches, but to such a little baby it may feel like miles.

Once the joey is safe in the pouch, it nurses and grows slowly. At about six months or so, it will leave the pouch for the first time. By ten months, it's old—and big—enough to leave permanently and travel on longer but far less tough journeys.

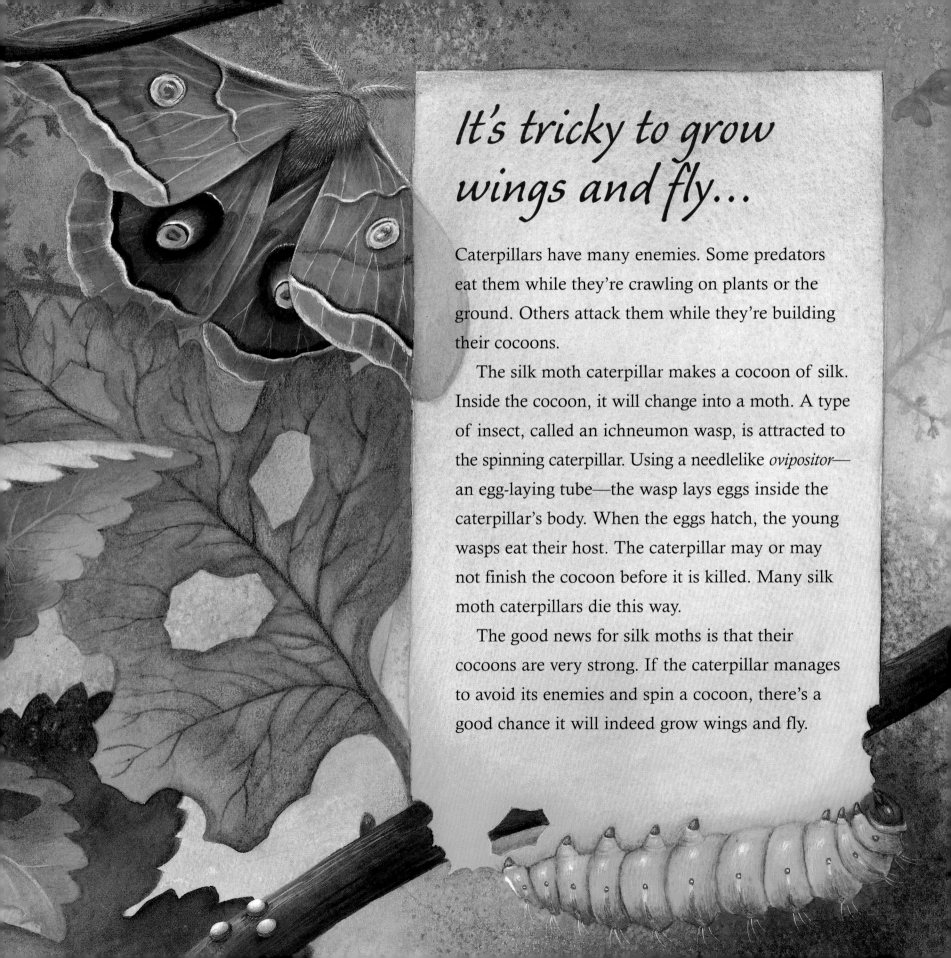

It's tricky to grow wings and fly...

Caterpillars have many enemies. Some predators eat them while they're crawling on plants or the ground. Others attack them while they're building their cocoons.

The silk moth caterpillar makes a cocoon of silk. Inside the cocoon, it will change into a moth. A type of insect, called an ichneumon wasp, is attracted to the spinning caterpillar. Using a needlelike *ovipositor*—an egg-laying tube—the wasp lays eggs inside the caterpillar's body. When the eggs hatch, the young wasps eat their host. The caterpillar may or may not finish the cocoon before it is killed. Many silk moth caterpillars die this way.

The good news for silk moths is that their cocoons are very strong. If the caterpillar manages to avoid its enemies and spin a cocoon, there's a good chance it will indeed grow wings and fly.

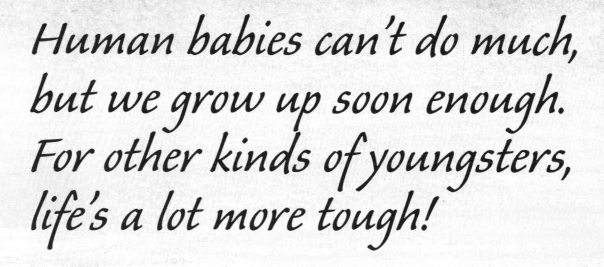

Human babies can't do much, but we grow up soon enough. For other kinds of youngsters, life's a lot more tough!

It's hard being a human baby. You can't walk. You can't talk. You can't do much of anything except eat and sleep. Until you're around six weeks old, your neck muscles are too weak and your head is too heavy to hold up straight. Until you're six months old or so, you can't sit up by yourself. During the long time that you're a baby, you have to rely on your parents to take care of all your needs.

On the other hand, if you're healthy and have caring parents, enough food, and good shelter, it isn't hard being a baby at all. You don't have to use your energy just to survive. Instead you can use it to grow physically and to develop your mind, your interests, and your personality. You can take the time to become you.

Compared with many other babies, we humans really have it easy.

Did you know that...

Freshwater **eels** live in rivers and lakes. But they travel to oceans to lay their eggs. As soon as they hatch, the baby eels must start the long journey back to freshwater. They cover thousands of miles over one to three years. At first the babies are small and transparent. They have no fins and can't swim, so they drift. Many get eaten by larger fish or die of the cold. The survivors undergo lots of changes during their trip. They grow teeth and fins and their skin turns dark and slimy. They face new dangers, such as fishermen or dams that block their waterways. At last some eels reach home. Years later they'll return to the ocean to have their own world-traveling babies.

Flamingos build nests—mounds of mud, straw, feathers, and stones—in lakes that have a high amount of *soda*, a powdery, saltlike combination of minerals. Each nest has one chick. If the water level is too high, the chicks may drown. If it's too low, the chicks' legs get coated with the soda and they may be unable to walk and feed themselves. Though other birds visit these lakes, only flamingos are born in them.

Hornbill chicks begin life in a tree hole. Their parents have plastered up the entrance with mud to form a barricade to protect the babies from predators. Among some types of hornbills, the mother breaks out when the chicks are half-grown. The babies patch up the barricade themselves and their parents feed them through a slit. When they're old enough to fly, the chicks break out of the nest, too.

A **golden eagle** usually has just two babies. They hatch in a nest high on a cliff, on a mountain, or up in a tree. Parent eagles feed their chicks meat. Sometimes both chicks thrive. But other times, the bigger, firstborn chick kills the other baby or forces it to starve. Perhaps having a sibling is a test of strength for an eaglet. The toughest babies are the ones most likely to become mighty hunters, just like their parents.

Baby **sand tiger sharks** don't just kill their siblings—they eat them. And they do it before they're born. Sand tiger shark mothers produce many eggs, which can become *embryos*—developing babies. The embryos eat the eggs and each other inside their mother until just two are left. Those two fine young cannibals are born about two and a half feet long, and are ready, willing, and able to catch any prey that comes their way.

Baby animals such as puppies and kittens spend a lot of time with their mothers and nurse often. But other baby animals don't. Mother **rabbits**, which eat grass and leaves, and **tree shrews**, which eat insects and worms, don't stay with their young. Baby rabbits are fed just once every night. Baby tree shrews are fed once every few *days*. Their meal has to be extremely nutritious and last them a long time.

Baby **swifts** are also left alone while their parents search for insects. If their parents are gone for a long period, the chicks' temperature drops very low and they fall into a deep sleep. They will wake when food is available again.

Giraffes are the tallest animals in the world. Mother giraffes give birth standing up. That means when it's born, a baby giraffe drops almost a full six feet to the ground—headfirst. Most babies survive the fall. But within an hour, a baby giraffe must get up on its feet and nurse. Within half a day, it must run, otherwise it won't be able to escape predators. Giraffe mothers take good care of their young. But if a baby is too weak to stand, the mother may abandon it. It takes a tough baby to join the herd, flee from danger, and grow into a tall and strong grown-up giraffe.

Lion cubs live in large groups called *prides*. They usually have devoted parents. But sometimes outsider males want to take over a pride. They chase away the resident males and kill their cubs. Then the conquering males will mate with the females and have new cubs of their own.

Mother **deer** and **seals** leave their fawns and pups in the woods and on the beach when they go off in search of food. Well-meaning but misinformed people sometimes take the youngsters away when they should leave them alone. Then the babies may have to spend their lives in zoos and wildlife centers instead of in the wild.